QUALITY IMPROVEMENT IN RESPIRATORY CARE

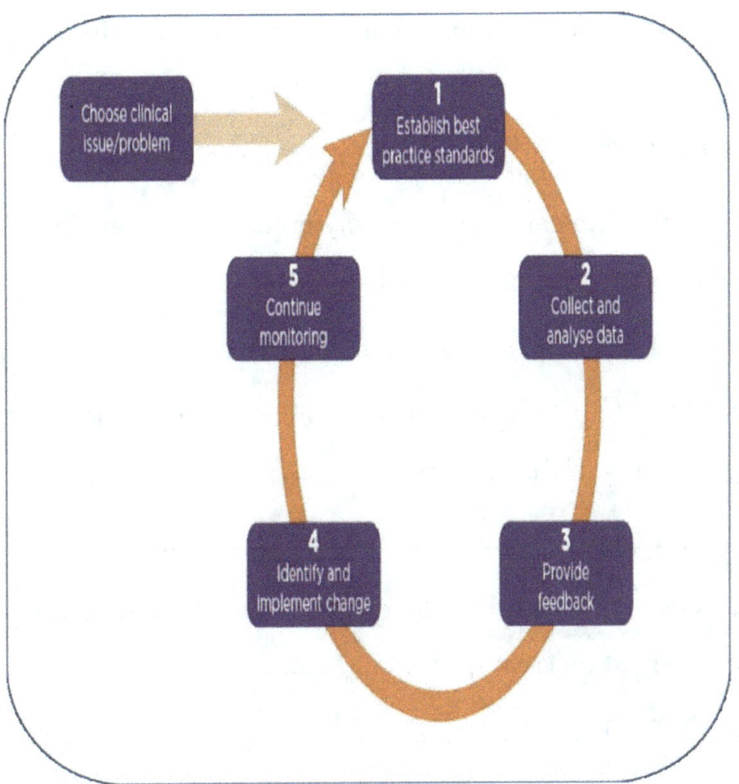

TABLE OF CONTENTS

INTRODUCTION

In the ever-evolving landscape of healthcare, quality improvement (QI) stands as a pivotal element for enhancing patient outcomes and optimizing care processes. Specifically within the realm of respiratory care, understanding and implementing QI strategies is essential for healthcare providers, including respiratory therapists, physicians, and nurses. This book, "Elevating Excellence: A Comprehensive Guide to Quality Improvement in Respiratory Care," aims to bridge the knowledge gap regarding QI in respiratory care, offering a comprehensive overview of key concepts, methodologies, and practical applications.

Respiratory care is critical in managing a range of conditions, from chronic obstructive pulmonary disease (COPD) to pneumonia and asthma. With the complexities of respiratory disorders, a dedicated focus on quality improvement can lead to significant advancements in patient safety, treatment efficacy, and overall care quality. This book is designed to equip healthcare professionals with the necessary tools and insights to enhance the quality of care delivered to patients.

By the end of this book, healthcare providers will have a comprehensive understanding of quality improvement in respiratory care, empowering them to enhance their practice and, ultimately, improve patient outcomes. Together, we can elevate the standard of care in respiratory medicine, ensuring that every patient receives the highest quality treatment possible.

MODULE ONE

LESSON: UNDERSTANDING QUALITY IMPROVEMENT IN RESPIRATORY CARE

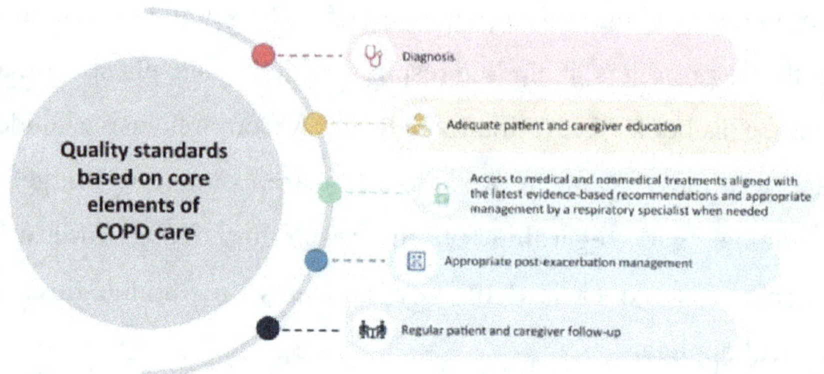

Quality Improvement (QI) has emerged as a crucial component of healthcare delivery, fundamentally reshaping how providers approach patient care. This lesson will explore the foundational concepts of QI, specifically within the context of respiratory care, highlighting its importance and relevance to healthcare providers.

Defining Quality Improvement

At its core, quality improvement refers to systematic efforts to enhance patient care and outcomes. It involves continuous evaluation and enhancement of processes, aiming to achieve higher standards of healthcare delivery. In respiratory care, this encompasses improving diagnostic accuracy, optimizing treatment protocols, and ensuring patient safety.

The Role of Quality Improvement in Healthcare

The implementation of QI initiatives has been shown to lead to significant advancements in patient outcomes. By systematically analyzing care processes, healthcare providers can identify areas of inefficiency or inaccuracy, thus implementing changes that enhance the overall quality of care. **The primary goals of QI in healthcare include:**

- Enhancing Patient Safety: Reducing the risk of errors and adverse events during patient care.
- Improving Clinical Outcomes: Focusing on achieving better health outcomes for patients through evidence-based practices.
- Increasing Efficiency: Streamlining care processes to minimize waste and reduce costs.
- Promoting Patient Satisfaction: Ensuring that patients have positive experiences during their care journey.

Key Components of Quality Improvement

To effectively implement QI initiatives, healthcare providers must understand several key components:

- Data-Driven Decision Making: QI relies heavily on data collection and analysis. Providers must gather relevant data on patient outcomes, care processes, and performance metrics to identify areas needing improvement. This data-driven approach allows for informed decision-making and targeted interventions.

- Teamwork and Collaboration: Effective QI requires a collaborative approach. Multidisciplinary teams, including respiratory therapists, physicians, and nurses, must work together to implement changes. This collaboration fosters communication, enhances problem-solving capabilities, and ensures that all perspectives are considered in the decision-making process.

- Patient-Centered Care: Quality improvement initiatives must prioritize the needs and preferences of patients. Engaging patients in their care, seeking their feedback, and involving them in decision-making are crucial for ensuring that care is tailored to individual needs.

- Continuous Learning and Adaptation: QI is an ongoing process that necessitates a culture of continuous learning. Healthcare providers should regularly evaluate the effectiveness of implemented changes, seeking opportunities for further improvement and adapting strategies as necessary.

Importance of Quality Improvement in Respiratory Care

Respiratory care encompasses a wide range of conditions, including asthma, COPD, pneumonia, and pulmonary fibrosis. Given the complexity of these conditions, a dedicated focus on quality improvement is paramount. Some key reasons why QI is particularly important in respiratory care include:

- High Prevalence of Respiratory Diseases: Respiratory diseases are among the leading causes of morbidity and mortality worldwide. Implementing QI initiatives can significantly impact patient outcomes and reduce the burden of these conditions.

- Complex Treatment Protocols: Effective respiratory care often involves a multidisciplinary approach, requiring collaboration among various healthcare providers. Quality improvement fosters teamwork, ensuring that all members of the care team are aligned in their efforts to optimize patient care.

- Rapid Advancements in Evidence-Based Practices: The field of respiratory care is continually evolving, with new treatments and guidelines emerging regularly. QI initiatives allow healthcare providers to stay current with the latest evidence and incorporate these advancements into their practice.

- Patient Safety Concerns: Respiratory procedures, such as intubation and mechanical ventilation, carry inherent risks. Quality improvement efforts can help minimize these risks through standardized protocols, staff training, and monitoring systems.

MODULE TWO

LESSON: CLINICAL SIGNS AND SYMPTOMS: RECOGNIZING QUALITY INDICATORS IN PATIENTS

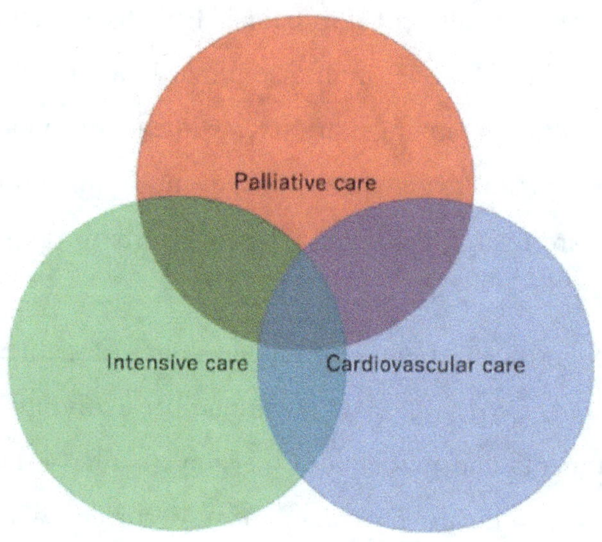

In the field of respiratory care, clinical signs and symptoms are essential indicators of a patient's health status and the effectiveness of treatment interventions. Recognizing these signs and symptoms allows healthcare providers to identify potential complications, assess the severity of respiratory conditions, and determine the necessary quality improvement strategies. This lesson will delve into the various clinical indicators relevant to respiratory care, highlighting their significance in monitoring patient outcomes and enhancing the quality of care.

Importance of Clinical Signs and Symptoms in Respiratory Care

Clinical signs and symptoms serve as critical data points that inform healthcare providers about a patient's respiratory status. These indicators help in:

- Diagnosis: Accurate diagnosis is paramount in respiratory care. Clinical signs such as shortness of breath, wheezing, and cough can guide providers in identifying specific respiratory conditions, allowing for timely interventions.

- Monitoring Treatment Efficacy: By regularly assessing clinical signs and symptoms, healthcare providers can evaluate the effectiveness of treatment plans. Notable improvements or deteriorations in symptoms can inform necessary adjustments to therapy.

- Identifying Complications: Respiratory conditions can lead to various complications, including respiratory failure and pneumonia. Recognizing clinical signs early can facilitate prompt intervention and prevent further deterioration.

- Guiding Quality Improvement Initiatives: Clinical indicators provide valuable data for quality improvement efforts. Analyzing patterns in symptoms can help identify trends, informing the development of evidence-based protocols and interventions.

KEY CLINICAL SIGNS AND SYMPTOMS

1. Dyspnea (Shortness of Breath)

Dyspnea is one of the most common and distressing symptoms experienced by patients with respiratory conditions. It can range from mild discomfort to severe respiratory distress. Understanding the severity and pattern of dyspnea is critical for assessing a patient's respiratory status.

- Assessment: Providers should evaluate dyspnea using scales, such as the Borg Rating of Perceived Exertion, to quantify the severity. Additionally, assessing the patient's ability to perform daily activities can provide insight into the impact of dyspnea on their quality of life.
- Quality Improvement Implications: Monitoring dyspnea levels over time can identify trends that may indicate the need for treatment adjustments, such as increasing bronchodilator therapy or initiating supplemental oxygen.

2. Cough

Coughing is a protective reflex that helps clear secretions from the airways. However, a persistent or chronic cough can indicate underlying respiratory issues.

- Assessment: Providers should assess the character of the cough (dry vs. productive), frequency, and associated symptoms (e.g., hemoptysis). A detailed history can help distinguish between acute and chronic cough, guiding further evaluation.

- Quality Improvement Implications: Documenting cough characteristics can help identify patients at risk for exacerbations or complications, prompting early intervention and targeted education regarding cough management strategies.

3. Sputum Production

Sputum production can provide valuable information regarding the presence of infection or inflammation in the respiratory system.

- Assessment: The volume, color, and consistency of sputum should be documented. Purulent sputum may indicate infection, while clear sputum may suggest other underlying issues.

- Quality Improvement Implications: Monitoring sputum characteristics can help healthcare providers identify patients requiring antibiotic therapy or further diagnostic evaluation, contributing to improved management of respiratory conditions.

4. Chest Pain

Chest pain can be a significant indicator of respiratory issues, especially in conditions such as pulmonary embolism or pneumonia.

- Assessment: Providers should assess the quality, location, and duration of chest pain, along with associated symptoms (e.g., shortness of breath). It is essential to differentiate between respiratory and cardiac causes of chest pain.

- Quality Improvement Implications: Early recognition of chest pain associated with respiratory conditions can lead to prompt interventions, such as imaging studies or the initiation of anticoagulation therapy.

5. Cyanosis

Cyanosis, or bluish discoloration of the skin and mucous membranes, is a critical sign of inadequate oxygenation and should be promptly assessed.

- Assessment: Peripheral and central cyanosis should be distinguished, as peripheral cyanosis can result from conditions affecting circulation rather than respiratory status.

- Quality Improvement Implications: Recognizing cyanosis can prompt immediate interventions, such as administering supplemental oxygen or assessing for respiratory failure, improving patient safety and outcomes.

Recognizing Trends in Clinical Indicators

For effective quality improvement in respiratory care, healthcare providers must recognize trends in clinical indicators over time. By consistently monitoring and documenting symptoms, providers can:

- Identify Patterns: Analyzing trends in symptoms can help identify patterns that may indicate the need for quality improvement initiatives. For example, a rising trend in dyspnea among patients with COPD may warrant the implementation of enhanced education and management strategies.

- Facilitate Communication: Consistent documentation of clinical signs and symptoms promotes effective communication among healthcare team members, ensuring that all providers are aware of a patient's status and treatment needs.

- Empower Patient Engagement: Educating patients about the importance of reporting their symptoms and recognizing changes in their condition can enhance their engagement in the care process, contributing to better outcomes.

LESSON: PHYSIOLOGICAL ASSESSMENTS: THE HEART OF QUALITY IMPROVEMENT IN RESPIRATORY CARE

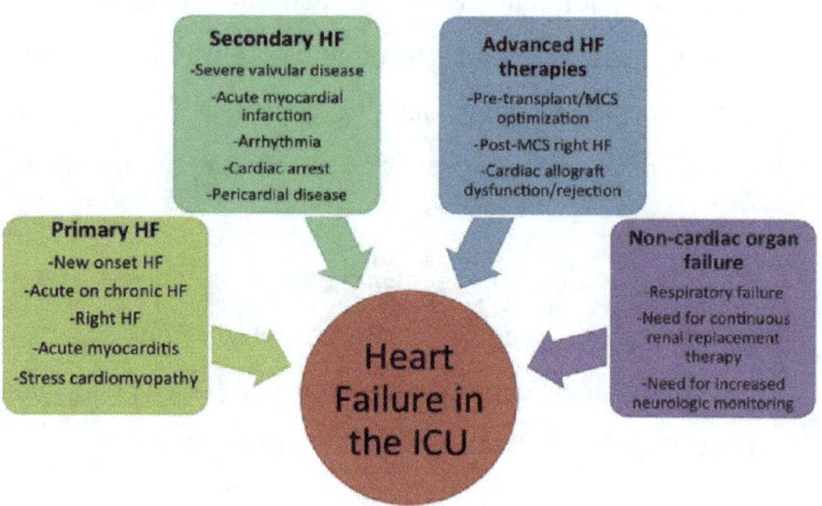

Physiological assessments are essential for evaluating respiratory function and guiding clinical decision-making in respiratory care. This lesson will focus on key physiological parameters that healthcare providers must assess, emphasizing their role in quality improvement and patient safety.

Importance of Physiological Assessments

Physiological assessments provide critical information about a patient's respiratory status and overall health. By measuring key indicators, healthcare providers can:

- Evaluate Respiratory Function: Assessing physiological parameters allows providers to determine the severity of respiratory conditions and monitor changes over time.

- Guide Treatment Decisions: Physiological assessments inform clinical decision-making, helping providers tailor treatment plans to individual patient needs.

- Monitor Treatment Efficacy: Regular assessments enable providers to evaluate the effectiveness of interventions, ensuring that patients receive optimal care.

- Identify Early Signs of Deterioration: Timely physiological assessments can help identify early signs of respiratory distress or failure, allowing for prompt interventions to improve patient outcomes.

KEY PHYSIOLOGICAL ASSESSMENTS

1. Respiratory Rate (RR)

The respiratory rate is a fundamental vital sign that indicates the number of breaths a patient takes per minute. Abnormal respiratory rates can signify various respiratory conditions, such as hypoxia or hypercapnia.

- Assessment: Normal respiratory rates typically range from 12 to 20 breaths per minute in adults. Rates outside this range should be further evaluated to determine the underlying cause.

- Quality Improvement Implications: Monitoring trends in respiratory rates can help identify patients at risk for respiratory failure or exacerbations, prompting timely interventions and adjustments in treatment plans.

2. Oxygen Saturation (SpO2)

Oxygen saturation measures the percentage of hemoglobin saturated with oxygen, providing insight into a patient's oxygenation status.

- Assessment: Pulse oximetry is a non-invasive method for measuring SpO2. Normal levels typically range from 95% to 100%. Values below this range indicate potential hypoxemia and require further evaluation.
- Quality Improvement Implications: Regularly monitoring SpO2 levels can help healthcare providers identify patients needing supplemental oxygen or other interventions, ensuring optimal oxygenation and reducing the risk of complications.

3. Arterial Blood Gases (ABGs)

ABG analysis provides comprehensive information about a patient's respiratory and metabolic status, including oxygen and carbon dioxide levels, pH, and bicarbonate.

- Assessment: ABG results help providers assess respiratory function, identify acid-base imbalances, and evaluate the effectiveness of oxygen therapy.
- Quality Improvement Implications: Regular ABG monitoring in at-risk patients can help guide treatment decisions and

prompt timely interventions, enhancing the quality of care and patient safety.

4. Peak Expiratory Flow Rate (PEFR)

PEFR measures the maximum speed of expiration, providing valuable information about airway function and potential obstruction.

- Assessment: PEFR is often used in asthma management to assess the severity of airway obstruction. Providers should establish baseline values for patients with known respiratory conditions to monitor changes over time.
- Quality Improvement Implications: Monitoring PEFR can help healthcare providers identify exacerbations early, allowing for prompt interventions to improve airway function and prevent hospitalizations.

5. Lung Auscultation

Auscultation of lung sounds is a critical component of respiratory assessments, providing insight into airway patency and potential complications.

- Assessment: Providers should listen for normal and abnormal lung sounds, including wheezing, crackles, and rhonchi. Documenting these findings can help identify changes in the patient's condition.
- Quality Improvement Implications: Regular lung auscultation can help healthcare providers detect early signs of respiratory

distress, enabling timely interventions to improve patient outcomes.

Integrating Physiological Assessments into Quality Improvement Initiatives

To maximize the benefits of physiological assessments in respiratory care, healthcare providers should integrate these evaluations into their quality improvement initiatives:

- Standardizing Assessment Protocols: Developing standardized protocols for conducting physiological assessments ensures consistency in data collection and interpretation. This standardization allows for more accurate comparisons and evaluations over time.

- Utilizing Data for Performance Improvement: Collecting and analyzing data from physiological assessments can help identify trends and patterns that inform quality improvement initiatives. For example, a rise in abnormal $SpO2$ levels among a specific patient population may indicate the need for enhanced education or changes in management protocols.

- Fostering a Culture of Continuous Learning: Encouraging ongoing education and training for healthcare providers regarding the importance of physiological assessments promotes a culture of continuous learning. This culture ensures that providers remain current with best practices and emerging evidence.

- Engaging Patients in Their Care: Educating patients about the significance of physiological assessments and involving them in monitoring their respiratory status empowers them to take an active role in their care. This engagement can lead to improved outcomes and greater patient satisfaction.

MODULE FOUR

LESSON: THERAPEUTIC APPROACHES: BEST PRACTICES FOR QUALITY IMPROVEMENT IN TREATMENT

In respiratory care, therapeutic interventions play a crucial role in managing respiratory conditions and improving patient outcomes. This lesson will focus on evidence-based therapeutic approaches, emphasizing best practices for quality improvement in treatment strategies.

Importance of Therapeutic Interventions

Therapeutic interventions are essential for managing respiratory conditions, addressing symptoms, and improving overall health. The importance of these interventions can be summarized as follows:

- Symptom Management: Effective therapeutic interventions can alleviate symptoms such as dyspnea, cough, and wheezing, enhancing the patient's quality of life.

- Disease Control: Therapeutic approaches aim to control the underlying disease processes, preventing exacerbations and complications.

- Improving Functional Capacity: Optimizing therapeutic interventions can improve patients' functional capacity and ability to perform daily activities.

- Promoting Patient Safety: Evidence-based therapeutic interventions help reduce the risk of adverse events, ensuring that patients receive safe and effective care.

KEY THERAPEUTIC APPROACHES

1. Pharmacological Interventions

Pharmacological treatments are a cornerstone of respiratory care, and providers must understand the appropriate use of medications for managing respiratory conditions:

- Bronchodilators: Short-acting and long-acting bronchodilators are essential for managing conditions such as asthma and COPD. Understanding the appropriate indications and dosing is crucial for optimizing treatment.

- Corticosteroids: Inhaled corticosteroids are vital for controlling airway inflammation in asthma patients. Providers should be knowledgeable about the long-term effects and proper inhalation techniques to ensure therapeutic efficacy.

- Antibiotics: Appropriate use of antibiotics is essential in managing respiratory infections. Providers must be vigilant in identifying indications for antibiotic therapy while being mindful of antibiotic stewardship principles.

2. Non-Pharmacological Interventions

In addition to pharmacological treatments, non-pharmacological interventions are essential for improving respiratory health:

- Pulmonary Rehabilitation: This comprehensive program includes exercise training, education, and self-management strategies for patients with chronic respiratory diseases. Implementing pulmonary rehabilitation can significantly improve functional capacity and quality of life.

- Smoking Cessation Programs: Smoking is a leading cause of respiratory diseases. Implementing effective smoking cessation programs can reduce the incidence of respiratory conditions and enhance overall health.

- Patient Education: Educating patients about their conditions, treatment plans, and self-management strategies is vital for empowering them to take an active role in their care.

Integrating Therapeutic Approaches into Quality Improvement Initiatives

To maximize the benefits of therapeutic interventions in respiratory care, healthcare providers should integrate these approaches into their quality improvement initiatives:

- Developing Evidence-Based Protocols: Establishing evidence-based protocols for therapeutic interventions ensures that patients receive consistent and effective care. These protocols should be regularly reviewed and updated based on emerging evidence.

- Monitoring Treatment Efficacy: Regularly assessing treatment efficacy through follow-up evaluations and patient feedback can help identify areas for improvement and inform adjustments in therapy.

- Fostering a Culture of Collaboration: Encouraging interdisciplinary collaboration among healthcare providers enhances communication and coordination of care, leading to better patient outcomes.

- Engaging Patients in Shared Decision-Making: Involving patients in the decision-making process regarding their treatment plans promotes patient engagement and satisfaction. Providers should encourage discussions about treatment options and respect patient preferences.

MODULE FIVE

LESSON: MEDICATION MANAGEMENT: OPTIMIZING PHARMACOLOGICAL INTERVENTIONS IN RESPIRATORY CARE

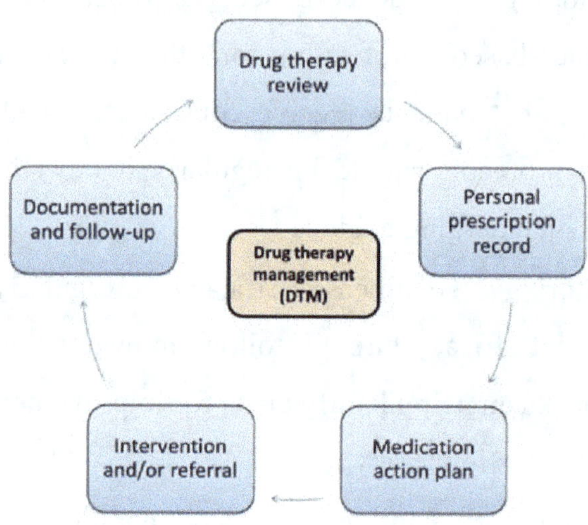

Medication management is a critical aspect of respiratory care, playing a vital role in optimizing treatment outcomes and ensuring patient safety. This lesson will focus on best practices for medication management in respiratory care, emphasizing the importance of optimizing pharmacological interventions.

Importance of Medication Management

Effective medication management is essential for achieving optimal therapeutic outcomes in respiratory care. The importance of medication management can be summarized as follows:

- Enhancing Treatment Efficacy: Proper medication management ensures that patients receive the most effective treatments for their respiratory conditions, improving overall health and well-being.

- Minimizing Adverse Effects: Vigilant medication management can help identify and mitigate potential adverse effects, ensuring patient safety during treatment.

- Promoting Adherence: Effective communication and education regarding medications can enhance patient adherence to treatment plans, leading to improved outcomes.

- Facilitating Interdisciplinary Collaboration: Medication management requires collaboration among healthcare providers, promoting a coordinated approach to patient care.

KEY COMPONENTS OF MEDICATION MANAGEMENT

1. Comprehensive Medication Review

A comprehensive medication review is essential for assessing a patient's medication regimen and identifying potential issues:

- Medication Reconciliation: Providers should conduct medication reconciliation at each patient encounter to ensure an accurate and up-to-date medication list. This process helps identify discrepancies and potential interactions.

- Assessing Indications and Dosing: Providers must evaluate the indications for each medication, ensuring that patients are prescribed appropriate therapies at the correct dosages.

2. Patient Education

Patient education is vital for ensuring that patients understand their medications and adhere to treatment plans:

- Medication Instructions: Healthcare providers should provide clear and concise instructions regarding medication administration, including inhaler techniques and timing.
- Addressing Concerns: Providers should encourage patients to express any concerns or questions regarding their medications, fostering open communication and trust.

3. Monitoring for Adverse Effects

Regular monitoring for potential adverse effects is essential for ensuring patient safety during medication therapy:

- Assessing Side Effects: Providers should routinely inquire about potential side effects experienced by patients and document any adverse reactions. This process allows for timely intervention and adjustments in therapy as needed.
- Utilizing Assessment Tools: Employing standardized assessment tools can facilitate the identification of medication-related issues and improve the overall quality of medication management.

Integrating Medication Management into Quality Improvement Initiatives

To optimize medication management in respiratory care, healthcare providers should integrate these practices into their quality improvement initiatives:

- Establishing Protocols for Medication Management: Developing standardized protocols for medication management ensures consistency in practice and adherence to evidence-based guidelines.

- Utilizing Technology for Medication Management: Implementing electronic health records and clinical decision support systems can enhance medication management by facilitating communication, documentation, and monitoring.

- Fostering Interdisciplinary Collaboration: Encouraging collaboration among healthcare providers, including pharmacists, can enhance medication management and ensure comprehensive care for patients.

- Engaging Patients in Self-Management: Educating patients about their medications and encouraging self-management strategies can empower them to take an active role in their care, improving adherence and outcomes.

CONCLUSION

Respiratory care is a critical component of healthcare, and ensuring its quality requires a multifaceted approach. This book has explored essential aspects of airway management, clinical assessments, imaging interpretation, therapeutic interventions, medication management, and recognizing respiratory condition manifestations. Throughout, the focus has been on best practices, evidence-based guidelines, and the integration of these practices into quality improvement initiatives.

Key strategies for maintaining and enhancing respiratory care include the use of standardized protocols, fostering interdisciplinary collaboration, engaging patients in their care, and emphasizing the importance of continuous learning and adaptation. By prioritizing patient safety, improving treatment efficacy, and staying current with evolving clinical evidence, healthcare providers can consistently deliver high-quality respiratory care.

Ongoing commitment to quality improvement is not just about addressing immediate clinical needs but about fostering a long-term culture of excellence. Through this commitment, respiratory care professionals can ensure better outcomes for patients, enhance their well-being, and contribute to the overall advancement of healthcare.

This book has provided a comprehensive guide to improving respiratory care practices, empowering healthcare providers to meet the highest standards of patient care.

<u>REFERENCES</u>

American Thoracic Society. (2017). *ATS/ERS guidelines for managing respiratory failure. American Journal of Respiratory and Critical Care Medicine.*

Bianchi, R., & Singer, M. (2019). *Respiratory management in critical care: From ventilation to advanced therapy. Critical Care Medicine.*

Blasi, F., & Aliberti, S. (2018). *Managing severe respiratory conditions: The role of medication management and therapy adherence.* The Lancet Respiratory Medicine.

Celli, B. R., & MacNee, W. (2018). *Standards for the diagnosis and treatment of patients with COPD: A guide for clinicians. European Respiratory Journal.*

Dellinger, R. P., Levy, M. M., & Rhodes, A. (2019). *Surviving sepsis campaign: International guidelines for management of sepsis and septic shock. Critical Care Medicine.*

Goldstein, R. S., & Hill, K. (2020). *Improving outcomes in respiratory therapy through patient-centered care and quality improvement. Journal of Pulmonary Rehabilitation.*

Henneman, E. A., & Gawlinski, A. (2020). *Strategies for quality improvement in respiratory care: The role of interdisciplinary collaboration and patient safety. American Journal of Nursing.*

Kacmarek, R. M., Stoller, J. K., & Heuer, A. J. (2020). *Egan's Fundamentals of Respiratory Care.*

Kollef, M. H., & Micek, S. T. (2019). *Ventilator-associated pneumonia: Clinical management and prevention strategies. Critical Care Clinics.*

Leatherman, S. T., Berwick, D. M., & Ivers, N. M. (2021). *Quality improvement in healthcare: Practical applications for providers and systems. Journal of Healthcare Quality.*